# beautifulbaskets

# beautifulbaskets
## decorating, entertaining, and collecting

text by Jeanine Larmoth

principal photography by Monica Buck

QVC PUBLISHING, INC.

QVC Publishing, Inc.
Jill Cohen, Vice President and Publisher
Ellen Bruzelius, General Manager
Sarah Butterworth, Editorial Director
Cassandra Reynolds, Publishing Assistant

Produced by Smallwood & Stewart, Inc., New York City
Editor, Alexia Meyers
Designer, Lynne Yeamans
Stylist, Amy Leonard
Photographs by The Peterborough Historical Society: pages 10-19;
Philip Flynn: pages 20-23; Monica Buck: all other pages

Published by QVC Publishing, Inc., 50 Main Street, Mt. Kisco, New York 10549

QVC Publishing books are available at special discounts when purchased in bulk for
premiums and sales promotions as well as for fund-raising or educational use. Special editions or
book excerpts can be created to specification. For details, contact the address below:

QVC Publishing
50 Main Street
Suite 201
Mt. Kisco, NY 10549

Manufactured in the United States of America

ISBN: 1-928998-34-8

First Edition

10 9 8 7 6 5 4 3 2 1

# contents

# foreword

Baskets are woven into our lives. Whether we realize it or not, they've probably been there all along. Maybe our first one was an Easter basket with green grass and pretty colored eggs, or the beautifully ribboned one we carried strewing rose petals before the bride, or the cradle made of bulrushes in the story of Moses. Perhaps it was the one we strapped to the bicycle we rode each day after school, or the one with everything from tablecloth to lemonade that our mother packed for picnics at the shore.

Baskets have always been workhorses, but they have also been part of pleasure and play. Of the many domestic objects we use around the house, no other takes on more diverse roles—or is regarded with more affection. This is because the basket still carries the imprint of the hands that have created it, have bent the supple wood and woven it, have learned from generations of those who have crafted baskets over time and around the world.

The people at the Peterboro Basket Company, in the rolling mountains of New Hampshire, are part of an organization that has been producing baskets for more than 150 years—baskets that are sturdy, handsome, ready to serve. The craft of basketmaking is part of their lives. The weavers respect the wood they work with and the tradition of the work they do. That sense of pride and satisfaction is embodied in every basket they make.

The pages of this book brim with ideas for incorporating their exquisite handmade creations into your life, from your daily routines to your most joyous celebrations. We hope it will inspire you to look at the humble basket in a whole new light and give you countless ways to simplify your chores and enrich your environment for years to come.

# a sense of history
## basketry and the origin of the peterboro basket company

Baskets are one of humanity's oldest artifacts, dating back at least 11,000 years to the Neolithic Age, a few centuries older than pottery. While much early earthenware is still admired behind glass cases in museums, the same is not often true of baskets. As utilitarian objects, they were worked until they fell apart. If they survive their millenia in hiding, they can be so well preserved that they look like recent antiques. Unlike products of most other crafts, which have changed over the centuries with the introduction of new techniques, today's baskets are created exactly as they were in the Stone Age.

The hardwood splint baskets of the Native Americans were the prototypes for the first settlers. Many knew how to make baskets, but the materials in the New World were different from those in England and Europe.

Later, the Algonquins taught the Shakers. In the Shakers' hands, the Algonquin baskets took on a new sense of elegance and balance. Though the work baskets they

All dressed up in bunting, "the world's largest basket" awaits Peterborough's Fourth of July parade in 1921. The proud cargo was made by the Eastern States Package Company, parent of today's Peterboro Basket Company.

made for their daily tasks at the marketplace were very sturdy, they contrived sewing baskets and pincushions dainty enough to please the ladies of nearby towns. The results of the Shakers' labors have never been surpassed, and their baskets remain some of America's most precious artifacts.

Ultimately, the skills of the basketmakers traveled West in Connestoga wagons packed to the hilt with the family's most beloved treasures—porcelains, a vintage family portrait—as well as the necessary iron pots and pans, the small, homespun wardrobes, and seeds for a new garden.

At their high point, baskets played an important role in the Arts and Crafts movement of the last part of the nineteenth century.

Alarmed by the onslaught of industry and inspired by the Centennial Exposition of 1876, ladies set out to beautify their homes with the creations of their own hands. Their perception of the importance of the handmade and of the craft of basketmaking foretold today's recognition of baskets.

Then, in the 1970s, after more than half a century of losing ground to paper bags, tin cans, corrugated cardboard, and plastic, baskets emerged as part of a new trend towards natural cooking and decorating. Previously regarded as useful but often discardable objects, baskets began to be valued as a form of traditional artwork that added to a sense of home.

Whole sections in department stores burgeoned with baskets. Along

rural highways, antiques stores hung them from walls and rafters. At the holidays and on other special occasions, baskets climbed to the top of wish lists, both as presents themselves or as attractive ways of offering them.

Since then, baskets have only increased in popularity. What gives baskets near infinite variety are the materials and techniques of different cultures. Materials in the tropics may be fibrous tree barks, rope-like vines, or wide leaves that shade the forest floor. In the Far East, the material could be bamboo; in Alaska, kelp; in Ecuador, palm fronds; in Tunisia, reeds.

A weaver and his work: In 1910, an employee of the Needham Basket Company leans on a stack of unfinished market baskets, used for leaf gathering and for holding fabric in textile factories.

Throughout the southern United States, the most precious baskets are those made from vines: curling tendrils of ivy, wisteria, honeysuckle, and wild grape or blackberry. Farther north, selection is made from deciduous trees such as birch, cedar, hazel, white pine, black walnut, or mulberry. Roots are another alternative, as well as grass, leaves, pine needles, rye, even the leaves of the yucca.

If the choice of materials is awe-inspiring, the uses to which baskets have been put are almost more so. The art of basketry has yielded rattan furniture, Panama hats, the fisherman's creel, screens, walls, rafts, corrals, basket lifts for miners, fish traps, sieves, thatched roofs, frames for the bearskin hats of Her Majesty's House Guards, huts that stand on stilts over water, and towering church spires. Roman chariots, helmets, and shields, and later, carriages and a rocking horse for Queen Victoria's children, were made of woven materials. The first sports cars in the smarter styles had side panels of wickerwork.

Color also is a way of distinguishing baskets. In the past, this was done by weaving together sweet grass, rice straw, cane, reeds, leaves, and bark to create subtle tapestries. Later, natural dyes were developed and the basketmaker rubbed them on the materials before weaving. Steeped in water, walnut bark gave off a black dye; boiled logwood chips, a yellow-brown; pokeberry, a red-purple; the iris, a shade of purple almost as dark as the flower itself.

Some of the most effective dyework is evidenced in the designs of Native American cultures. It is clear that their baskets were not always throwaways. Finely crafted ones played integral parts in ceremonies: A jagged line like lightening refers to the eternal power of the incoming tide; a spider spinning its web, a prayer for rain; stars in a circle, the constellation Corona.

Appreciated now as artful objects, baskets have become sought-after collectibles. Perhaps even more importantly they're an expected part of daily life, with the current insistence on the natural and environmentally pure. For instance, how much more appealing are eggs nesting in a basket on a refrigerator shelf? Winter's holly arching from a basket? Even the cat naps more cozily in an airy basket. Whatever lies ahead, the basket makes the trip more fun. And whatever task it's put to, a basket's sure to do it well.

# the peterboro basket
## a hallmark becomes an institution

The most familiar and possibly the oldest basket still in use in New England is the wooden splint basket. From roadside farmstands to the supermarket, the splint bushel basket overflows with the season's temptations: tasseled green-sheathed ears of sweet corn; polished purple or white eggplant; orange, green, and yellow squash; onions in golden skins; apples; and sweet potatoes. In summer, smaller, bent-splint baskets offer precious raspberries and juicy blackberries, strawberries, gooseberries, and black currants. In autumn, traditional oval baskets appear mounded with frosted blue Concord grapes.

Splint baskets are treasured for the gentler way of life they recall. Loaded to the rim and stored in cellars, they once meant security and bounty to be treasured through the long winter. Or on fierce days of ice and snow, when the wind snapped like a sail, big baskets were filled and carried over the miles to a neighbor down the road. On Saturday night, splint baskets became bearers of satisfying pots of hot baked beans from the bake shop or of still-warm pies prepared for a church social.

The art of neighborliness was built into the splint baskets. Native Americans led the settlers into the woods to point out the indigenous ash they themselves cut to make baskets. Sturdy yet pliable ash can be bent without breaking and is easily peeled into long, thin strips. To get splints, they pounded the logs' growth rings with wooden mallets to loosen the layers. This method for separating the splints is much the same today.

Ash splints can be sliced again and again until they're a little thicker than a heavy thread. A popular

Surrounded by his coworkers, and one idler, a mustachioed weaver, pictured at Needham's factory in 1910, prepares to nail the bottom of a bushel basket as it rests sideways on a form. The vertical splints are called uprights, or staves.

Shaker basket, based on one made by the Penobscot Indians of Maine, was the porcupine, or the birthday, basket—a fantasy of curled, paper-thin splints. Today, the Appalachian ash is the tree of choice for splint baskets. Found scattered through low-lying woods, the trees are harvested throughout the year in Vermont and New Hampshire.

One of the leading buyers of ash wood planks is the Peterboro Basket Company in Hillsborough County, New Hampshire. For Peterboro, the wood must be top grade: flexible, green wood without fault, with a straight grain and no knots. The oldest manufacturer of splint baskets in the country, the Peterboro Basket Company began almost 150 years ago as a firm established by a former lead pipe maker, Amzi Childs. In 1854, after thirteen years in Peterborough, Childs began to see possibilities in basketmaking and stopped producing lead pipe. When his shop burned down in 1891, a frustrated Childs sold the business to a basket factory in nearby Milford.

In that same year, Henry B. Needham, a former foreman and superintendent for Childs, began his own basket factory in Peterborough. Only two years later, Needham was successful enough to start building a new three-story factory. The company prospered until 1915, when Needham became ill. His property was sold at auction to John W. Derby of The Peterborough Improvement Society. Derby, in turn, sold it to the Eastern States Package Company of Buffalo, New York. Though the building served until 1920, the unreliability of water power supplied by the Phoenix Mill Complex on the Contoocook River caused the Peterborough Company to commission the building of another factory. Fire once again changed the company's course in 1926. Rising from the ashes, the new Peterboro Basket Company began operating with the plant and equipment of the Eastern States Package Company. Other basketmaking competitors emerged from time to time, but in the end, only the Peterboro Basket Company remained.

What a 34-bushel basket can hold: Twelve men, workers at Needham's factory in 1911, fit, standing, into the giant basket. On the steps is the boss, Henry Needham, onetime foreman for Amzi Child, who eventually became immortalized as the "dean of basket manufacturers."

34 BUSHELS
MADE BY THE H.B. HESSMAN BASKET CO. PETERBORO N.H.

# walter hood, the face of tradition

Since 1983 the Peterboro Basket Company has been owned by the Dodds family. Russell and Joan Dodds and their children Wayne and Linda Murdock are all active in the business and are committed to keeping the Peterboro tradition alive. The busy factory is flooded with light and occupied by an assemblage of old iron machinery. Planers smooth the planks, ripsaws cut handles, cutting machines prepare the thin strips, and the slasher cuts the uprights. The factory is divided into several work areas: rooms for sanding, silk-screening, and for dipping completed baskets in vats of stain; the hooping area, where workers add the finishing splints, and a band saw, where they cut basket lids.

One of the most valued of the valued employees at Peterboro is Walter Hood. Raised in New Hampshire, Walter went from farming to making boxes before coming to the Peterboro Basket Company. Walter now makes baskets for demonstrations, crafts the frames that baskets are shaped on, designs baskets, conducts tours, and repairs the old machines. Two familiar Peterboro baskets, the

Walter Hood—dean of the Peterboro weavers—stands at his bench, opposite, one of few machines involved in crafting baskets. The cast-iron wheel is there for balance. The bench holds an oval weaving form, right, which rotates as he inserts the horizontal splints between the uprights.

Hood weaves the filler, ash splints made supple by steaming and soaking, left. Opposite, he stands with one of the tools of his trade: the hammer with which he adds the finishing hoops. Other necessities: a knife to cut off the ends of the filling, and his little wooden box of nails.

heart-shaped and the step basket, are Walter's imaginative designs. Hood's wife, Lillian, who also works at Peterboro, has created her own signature basket. Mrs. Hood put together two vegetable baskets and joined them with a hinge. The end product is an ample file basket with a sturdy lid.

The Hoods' home is chock-a-block with baskets, and the keynote is wood. The house is heated by wood, and Walter crafts wooden furniture. This passion has fueled him through fifty years of basketmaking. "I'm probably the only one here who knows the definition of 'basket.' When I first began working at Peterboro, I looked up the meaning in Webster's dictionary," he explains.

A "basket" literally is a receptacle made of interwoven materials. Naturally, the basket's practical purposes are also part of the charm. "You start with a lot of pieces," he says, "and they come together into something you can use."

Beauty and function: the duel traditions on which Peterboro was founded and on which legend is based. It is said that Peterboro baskets have traveled with American explorers to the ends of the earth and even traveled to New York City where, in the 1930s, they were used by workers removing garbage from the subway tracks. It is rather fitting that these baskets continue to function as receptacles, true to their name to the very end.

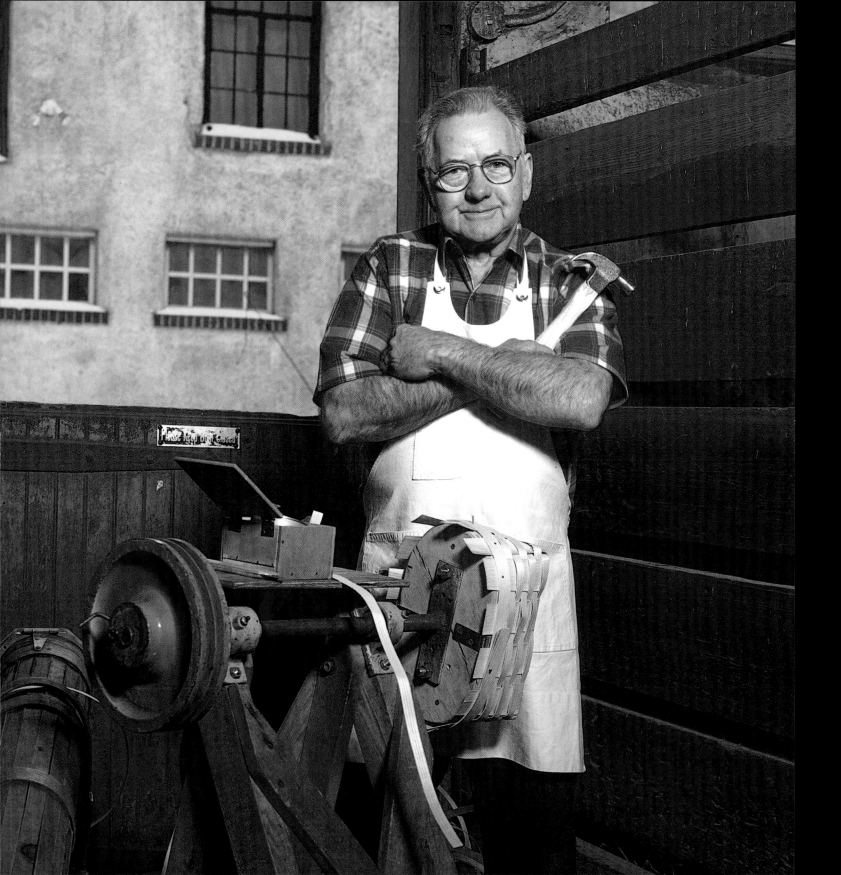

# chapter one

# the everyday beauty of baskets

OUR HOMES ARE INCREASINGLY INUNDATED WITH MODERN TECHNOLOGY: televisions, digital clocks, computers, microwave ovens, electronic appliances. Furniture styles have changed through the years. Fabric is no longer made on a hand loom. Lightbulbs have replaced candles. Alone among all these domestic developments stands the basket, handcrafted as it has been since the first one that a human constructed, of all-natural materials, with painstaking care.

Baskets, whether they are empty, brimming with exquisite potpourri, heaped with a collection of toy cars, or housing a library of videos, continue to enchant us. They have adjusted to our lives, becoming handy in endless ways, gently reassuring us that the new technology we take so much for granted has not really changed us. They are a constant reminder to us that beauty resides in the simplest forms.

# living areas
## the fabric of daily life

The living room, family room, and sitting room are the activity centers of the house, rooms where family and guests tend to gather for relaxation and lively conversation. But these are deceptively utilitarian rooms, accommodating a wide range of possessions: magazines and newspapers, board games, telephone and address books—everything one might need close at hand. To keep these busy living spaces looking inviting and genuinely comfortable, the basket has no equal.

Next to the sofa or the easy chair, a basket stands by with the weekly television guide and remote controls just where they're needed. A basket with a lid stores the telephone and answering machine, keeping the tangle of cords neatly out of sight; for your cordless, an open-top basket gives easy access. A basket of embroidery on a bookshelf is safe from kitty's paws. Two baskets can store books: one with new, unread titles, the second with those that are headed back to the library.

A basket for newspaper clippings, catalogs, and recipes cut from magazines keeps these bits of paper firmly under control. And the gardener or home shopper who enjoys poring over possible purchases at her leisure collects all the catalogs that come in the daily mail in one basket.

The family fix-it person or the hobbyist, incapable of being idle even while watching a television program, has a basket with a lid full of the equipment needed to put a chair back together or start an antique clock running again. With the lid closed, the basket is an object of beauty, not a jumble of pliers, screws, and duct tape.

And if a member of the family just cannot pull away from the big game or a beloved old film, a flat, shallow basket converts effortlessly into a charming tray for serving lunch or dinner. There must, of course, be baskets of fruit or chocolate chip cookies for munching, and a newspaper recycling basket by the door for tidying up on Sunday evening. Certainly your puppy or kitten deserves a basket for all the whimsical items that strike the fancy of a pet everyday. Even extra throw pillows make a pretty display when piled topsy-turvy in a large utility basket. Or heap them into a basket with a lid left partially opened to reveal a flash of color or a shimmer of fabric.

Baskets have seasonal appeal, too. In winter, devote a basket to all those Christmas receipts, and have a second one for travel brochures to dream over for your next vacation. One experienced globe-trotter swears by her travel basket: She automatically puts her passport, airline tickets, hotel confirmations, camera, maps, itineraries, and all the notes she'll need into the basket. As her departure approaches, she checks that all is in order, then transfers everything to a tote for carry-on luggage. When she returns home, her passport goes back into the basket, ready and waiting for her next trip.

For a new twist on a traditional favorite basket, invert a wastepaper basket and place a tray, mirror, or large piece of colored tile on "top." You can then use it as an end table for mugs of tea and hot chocolate or simply as a stand to hold a gallery of miniature teacups, framed photographs, a vase of flowers, or your favorite collection.

Look around your own living room and you're sure to come up with half a dozen personalized ways for organizing and storing all your family's "stuff" in handsome baskets.

# delicate
# yet rugged

Though its history dates back to the beginning of civilization, the basket has evolved to meet changing needs. One of its greatest virtues is that it is a real workhorse, carrying and holding large rough-edged chunks of firewood and kindling. Pick a sturdy basket and load it up with tools, sports equipment, just about anything that you need to gather and transport in a carrier that's secure, and know that the basket will not splinter, or break.

On the other hand, a basket can gently cosset your most delicate needlework, silk lingerie, chiffon scarves, and hosiery. Carefully line it with a sturdy fabric to prevent snags and pulls, and with its lid, no sun will seep in to fade delicate colors.

# stretching the limits

Think a picnic hamper is just for picnics? That a roll basket should hold only rolls? That a berry basket is only for when the blueberries are ripe? Think again. Versatility is the name of the game with baskets. What might have been a market basket years ago can go to the office, filled with an enviable lunch for one. A berry basket works just as hard in the cutting garden, safely nestling fresh-cut flowers until they can be arranged indoors. And that picnic hamper makes a wonderful carrier for all of baby's toys and bottles.

## berry baskets

Long, shallow, and easily carried, the berry basket can serve breakfast in bed, collect fabric scraps, transport bedding plants out to the spring garden, hold dozens of matched pairs of chopsticks at a Chinese dinner, or carry the freshly baked cake and tea to the table.

## long roll baskets

Try this adaptable basket for bridge sets—the playing cards, score pads, and pencils—for watercolor sets and brushes, for bangle bracelets, and for serving thinly sliced quickbreads at teatime.

## bath hampers

How many homes now have more than one bathroom? Some of us are even lucky enough to have saunas and steamrooms. The bath hamper can hold any of the accoutrements for these activities. An outdoor shower caddy keeps shampoo, soap, lotion, and sponges, and with the lid down, all will stay dry in the early morning fog. Think of the bath hamper when you're off to the pool or beach as well, to carry magazines, sunscreen, sunglasses, and towels.

## bicycle baskets

Do you live in a climate too cold for bicycle riding part of the year? Your bicycle basket needn't gather dust when you can't ride. Mount it on the wall of the garage or mud room and fill it with cold-weather gear: the gloves you need to shovel snow, an extra pair of earmuffs, and some heavy-duty thermal socks.

## backpacks

Just as bicycle baskets have other uses in cold weather, so do backpacks. They are a wonderfully decorative element indoors: Carefully attached with the flat side to the wall, the backpack looks great filled with dramatic stems of bittersweet for autumn; in winter, branches of evergreen will infuse the air with the scent of pine. And in early spring, when the ground is still too cold for a picnic, bring the outdoors in with some sunny forsythia or cherry blossoms.

## sports crate

These heavy-duty, oversize baskets are usually filled with ski boots, volley balls, and baseball gloves. But they are equally adept at moving any kind of delicate pottery or china. Think of them, too, when you're helping your kids pack for college or camp.

# kitchen

## art & beauty on the menu

A basket's roots are truly in the kitchen, since one of its earliest tasks was gathering food and water. And while kitchen technology has certainly changed since the first basket was woven, no kitchen today is complete without a basket. Storing—and displaying—fresh food in baskets is more efficient and more hygienic than in plastic bags, and it's known to prolong the life of produce. Now, more like extensions of the refrigerator, baskets keep potatoes, onions, squash, and eggplant ready for hearty meals; apples, peaches, and pears at hand for luscious pies; and melons in the proper airy environment to encourage ripening.

If the kitchen is the place for storing food, then with a sunny windowsill it also becomes a fine spot for growing herbs such as oregano, rosemary, and mint, in a lined windowsill basket. Anyone who has had to buy a bunch of chives at the market when the recipe calls for only a half-teaspoon will appreciate the value of fresh-grown herbs in the depths of winter.

Small baskets are a perfect fit as recipe card holders. The chef can gather all those bits and pieces in one place: Grandmother's best recipes, new ones from magazines to try, others given by friends. Be sure to include a pad and pencil for making your shopping list.

## a pantry full of ideas

One look around the average kitchen will reveal plastic bags of produce, saucers with tea bags and packets of sugar substitute, chipped mugs stuffed with corkscrews and can openers, and any number of unsightly but regularly needed items. Now think of all those necessities organized into handsome baskets: A hot cup of tea is more tantalizing when the bags are tucked into a small basket rather than tangled together in a cardboard tea box. Four or five pencil baskets, each filled with forks, knives, spoons, and serving utensils, are a pleasing sight. A tall, round basket can hold any number of spatulas, wooden spoons, wire whisks, and other cooking tools you want to have nearby for food preparation.

# bedroom

## taking refuge from busy days

The bedroom is a retreat, a tranquil spot in which to unwind, a place that grants you reprieve from the pressures of the day, a haven in which to prepare for tomorrow. If your bedroom is a storeroom for laundry, sewing projects, office work, and endless to-do lists, chances are you are not finding the tranquility you crave. The solution: baskets. Replace those plastic laundry baskets with woven ones. Try a basket with a lid to keep sewing projects in order. Get a large basket to hold your briefcase, paperwork, and files. Keep lists and notes that you've written to yourself in a pretty bedside basket.

On any Sunday morning, whether it's the darkest day of winter or the brightest summery gem, one of the most luxurious ways to celebrate is to treat yourself to a lazy breakfast in bed. Bring in the weekend newspapers, heat up some fresh biscuits, add a dozen perfect strawberries or cherries, and brew up a pot of your best coffee or tea. A sweet flower in a bud vase will complete the tray. Put on your favorite music, fluff your pillows, climb back into bed, and count your blessings: Who could ask for anything more? (Well, perhaps someone who would prepare that tray for you!)

# bathroom

## chart a course for tranquil waters

There's no room in the house more devoted to the nurturing of the sensual spirit than the bathroom. Here, we bathe in warm waters scented with perfumed soaps, step out onto soft rugs, dry with plush towels. Yet no room makes this divine sensuality harder to achieve. The reason, of course, is the sharp, cold light of utilitarian fixtures and the harsh luster of the tiles and enamel bathtubs and sinks that are typical bathroom decor.

Some ways to counteract this sterility are flowing curtains, softer lighting—and the natural textures and colors of baskets. The more the merrier. A small picnic hamper can take care of all the luxuries that make bathing or showering a sensory experience: sponges, soaps, pumice stones, brushes. If your bathroom gets its fair share of sunlight, a feather-leaved fern or thriving ficus tucked into a basket adds to the feeling of a lush retreat.

Each child should have his or her own basket to hold shampoo and toys, including a rubber ducky. Baskets are excellent for utilitarian supplies— scouring powder, ammonia—keeping these usually unattractive packages out of sight and gathered together for quick, midweek touch-ups.

Baskets on vanities, on shelves, or hung from a cabinet or wall contain all the shaving paraphernalia, hair products and accessories, and toiletries for each member of the household— even if your household has sloppy teenagers. A sectioned basket filled with jelly jars becomes a novel container for cotton balls, swabs, and other communal bathroom items. Placed on the windowsill and filled with colored crystals, stones, or chunks of glass, the same basket is a delicate suncatcher.

If your storage space is limited or the room cries out for a spot of color, place a basket full of rolled-up towels and washcloths next to the shower or tub. A smaller version set next to the sink is great for pretty hand towels.

# five-minute solutions

Artfully arranged, baskets become conversation pieces, casual displays that are little still lifes in themselves, a way to bring vitality and humor to a room on short notice. An empty basket is transformed into a festive treat in mere minutes. An old-fashioned splint basket turns into a showpiece of color and bounty with crisp, just-picked apples waiting to be bitten into. Put it in an unexpected place—on the front porch, in the entryway, on a picnic table, or near the back door—so the children can snack while they take a break from playing in the yard.

## teddy bears

Children and adults alike are charmed by teddies. Collect the ones scattered around your house; their condition isn't that important—raggedy edges only make them more lovable. Pile them together in a basket for an adorable, endearing display.

## garden delights

Flowers and plants aren't the only botanicals whose charm should be showcased. When the broccoli, just brought home from the market, has a purplish tinge and the cauliflower is particularly snowy, there is no reason they can't be put together and shown off in a basket. In the autumn, pinecones can be married with pomegranates and placed beneath a hall mirror for an instant seasonal decoration.

## collections

Do you have an odd collection or two that doesn't lend itself easily to display? Perhaps vintage fabrics, antique buttons, flowers made by veterans for Memorial Day. Why not put each collection in a basket of its own?

## sudden guests

Uh-oh: Company's coming in half an hour. Take a few minutes and relax as you fill a basket with bright sunny lemons. If you don't have any citrus fruits, work with whatever you can find in the kitchen pantry: mushrooms, bell peppers, cherry tomatoes. If the look is abundant, your centerpiece will be a hit.

## baby bundles

At a first birthday party, pile a basket with alphabet blocks (for baby to play with when the party's over). Little baskets of marshmallow crispy treats are a party pleasure for older children.

## gingerbread kids

Arrange an army of iced gingerbread boys, girls, and even dogs in a long, flat basket. Sprinkle raisins and colorful gumdrops between the rows of cookies.

## paradise found

For a party with a tropical twist, fill a doorknob basket or a small standing basket with dozens of tiny paper parasols—some open, some closed—and watch your visitors grin.

# outdoors

## a warm welcome all year

The basket has a long history of hard-working outdoor activity. Newly raked leaves are piled up in bushel baskets. A gardener carries bulbs, seed packets, trowel, and secateurs in a small basket or brings in sheaves of daffodils or stacks of just-pruned branches of flowering quince abundantly overflowing in a long flat basket.

The chore of toting clean laundry to and from the line is made that much more pleasant by baskets. A mail basket can be filled with clothespins ready to be carried out and hung on a nail on a tree in the backyard. Rest a basket (with a handle) full of clothespins on the ground at your feet while you're working or tie it right on the line with a ribbon if the grass is wet and dewy.

Caddy baskets, laden with ice cubes and glasses of lemonade or iced tea in July, hot chai or mulled apple cider in October, can be carried to visitors on the patio or porch. Baskets sit at the foot of a ladder ready to bring in the harvest from the fruit trees.

One charming role of the basket outdoors is the May basket, once filled with flowers and hung surreptitiously on the doorknob by a shy suitor. Today, the doorknob basket sees more action, its contents changing with the season, the occasion, and your mood. When the home team plays, fill it with pennants. If you're hosting a bridal shower, tie name tags to roses or peonies and slip them into the basket so guests will be able to identify one another. On a significant birthday, create a big atmosphere with tiny helium-filled balloons tied onto sticks.

Even children's playthings can be remodeled by baskets. Outdoor toys can be placed in baskets for transport to the sandbox or the yard. Then the grass, dirt, or sand can be shaken out when it's time to come in at dusk.

Let your outdoor basket send a message everyday. Autumn leaves, spring daffodils, or August dahlias all say, "Come in, sit down, let's chat."

# chapter two

# the hospitality of baskets

A BASKET IS ALWAYS INVITING, WHETHER IT'S PART OF A CELEBRATION OR PARTY, OR holding popcorn fresh from the popper, bread warm from the oven, or a snack to nibble on until dinner is on the table. A basket is like an open door, a fire in the fireplace, the merry peal of the doorbell, the hostess's smile. It says that guests have been looked forward to and prepared for, that time has been reserved, a favorite recipe readied, flowers brought in from the garden, extra wood gathered for the fire.

A warm welcome is a small basket placed beside a guest's bed, holding books carefully chosen to please, a bedtime peppermint, a box of tissues, a glass and a carafe of water. A hearty welcome is a large basket holding a washcloth and towels rolled just so, a diminutive basket with a tiny bottle of shampoo, a travel-size tube of toothpaste, a sleep mask—everyday items your guest may have forgotten, presented by you with care.

# centerpieces

## jewels of nature

The basket garden is a true delight of nature. Choose your basket and your plant, and voilà: You have a garden in winter, a tiny landscape that previews the summer garden, or a little version of the garden of your dreams. The windowsill garden may be a bouquet basket with cut sunflowers, zinnias, or asters, or a plastic-lined bread basket crowded with pots of colorful primroses. During the winter holidays, forced narcissus bulbs flourish into delicate yet plucky wands that look outstanding in doorknob baskets, windowsill baskets, even bicycle baskets brought indoors for the winter. In January, look to bright chirpy flowers that promise the return of spring; in fact, from December to March, the colors of inexpensive flowering plants cheer up rooms that look out on gray winter landscapes. Once spring arrives, fill your baskets with the intensely perfumed bells of hyacinths or with swanlike creamy tulips.

Basket gardens do best in the right temperature and light conditions. But this is not to say they cannot be moved into more unconventional locations just for an evening or a weekend. On party tables, bedside tables, or in the powder room, a basket of flowering plants or fragrant herbs will hold its own with the most lavish floral

arrangement. As the flowers begin to fade, lift the pot from the basket and replace it with a younger plant that has an entirely different look. A popular new fashion is to fill your basket with a cut-to-fit rectangle of wheat grass, which grows thick and luxuriant and boasts an invigorating green color. Another idea is to fill the basket's liner with sand, then insert stalks of beach grass and sprinkle the sand with small shells or smooth beach glass.

Centerpieces for dining tables need follow just a few rules to be successful. Most important is height: If it's too tall, it will cut off guests's views of one another, inhibiting conversation.

Highly scented flowers are not good choices, either; their fragrance can overpower the aromas of the food you serve. Instead, place extravagant centerpieces or ones laden with highly perfumed flowers on entry tables, on pianos, and in other areas where food is not being served.

Even when the flowers in the garden are dormant, basket gardens on a polished dining room table, a side table in the hall, or damask-cloaked tables under a party tent can reflect the changes in the season. Golden santolina, wheat, and straw flowers composed in a rectangular basket are a sunny reminder of autumn days outdoors.

With a plastic liner, the same generous basket that holds dried flowers can present fresh-cut flowers and branches.

A fireplace has undeniable charm, and baskets artfully arranged on a mantel always attract the eye. Change displays seasonally, for entertaining or just for whim. Most designers suggest that an arrangement have a focal point, such as a tall, deep basket brimming with foliage, flowers, or fruit.

The mantel basket requires a few basics to make an effective impression. Florist's foam will anchor the stems and branches of dried arrangements; a fitted liner will hold all the water needed to keep the cut flowers fresh.

Abundance is one key to a mantel basket. Fill it as bountifully as you can; experiment with different kinds of greens, leaves, and shrubs to combine textures for visual interest. Scatter a few pieces of greens around the base of the basket, and for a special holiday like Christmas, add a group of cheerful dime-store snowmen and trees.

With fresh flowers, consider that the back of the basket, unless it is in front of a mirror, will not be seen. Build your centerpiece from taller and larger flowers in the center to shorter and smaller ones on the outside, and always be sure to keep an eye on the overall shape.

# portable table settings

Setting a pretty table involves a lot more than putting out plates and glasses. With the help of baskets, a beautifully laid table can be assembled in just a few minutes. By planning ahead—placing cutlery in the table basket when it's fresh from the dishwasher, folding napkins as soon as they come from the dryer and adding them to the basket—setting the table becomes an activity not only quickly accomplished, but one young children can do. A roll basket lined with a linen cloth is ready for muffins or breadsticks, and a long, shallow basket can carry pitchers of water, lemonade, or milk.

## casual supper

Saturday lunch and Sunday supper are two of the meals at which we relax and unwind. The table setting can reflect this attitude by including a casual basket filled with all the condiments your family loves: ketchup, mustard, relish, mayonnaise, vinaigrette, and tartar sauce. Keep the basket in the refrigerator until mealtime.

## picnics

The whole point of a picnic is to have fun. And while we enjoy watching the kids run and play, we don't want to worry about broken glass. Pack up only plastic cups and bottles of juice and sparkling water in a beverage basket, then relax!

## milk basket

How many kinds of milk do you have in your refrigerator? Some of us have regular, fat-free, half-and-half for coffee, chocolate milk, and perhaps even soy milk or milk for the lactose intolerant. Collect all these cartons in a basket that slips easily from refrigerator to table at breakfast or teatime.

## for favors

Children's birthday parties sometimes involve a "goodie bag," a traditional thank-you gift from the host or hostess to friends who have come for all the fun and cake. Instead of a paper bag, tuck your choices in a basket and tie on a tag with the child's name so the basket can serve as a place card as well.

## summer sack

During the summer afternoons we all enjoy so much, do you find yourself running back and forth between kitchen and pool or gazebo to fetch the salt, the napkins, an extra serving spoon? Put all these items together in a basket that is kept in a cupboard outdoors, and be prepared with everything you need.

# entertaining

## easy, simple, elegant

Preshow or postgame, when friends come over for a casual evening, baskets can certainly be part of the relaxed and homey atmosphere, symbols of the hospitality that you extend. They help to harmonize all the different kinds of food you'll want to serve, giving your party a pulled-together look. A plastic-lined basket holds enough buttery, salty popcorn to satisfy even the hungriest sports fans or television aficionados.

Set out several baskets of whatever's in demand—peanuts, pistachios, and potato chips—and you won't have to worry about the supply running low. A napkin-lined bread basket is perfect for celery, carrots, and bell pepper strips.

Serve guacamole and salsa dips in bowls set in little baskets, with deep baskets of tortilla chips alongside. Coolers, with their liners filled with ice, should be placed around the house, some with soda and juice, others with beer, and perhaps one with wine.

Desserts, too, are tremendously appealing when they are part of the basket motif. Consider a long basket with duel handles to hold cakes or pies. In winter, a bicycle basket can be hung on the wall near the fireplace, filled with marshmallows pushed onto sticks and ready to be toasted over the fire. After-dinner mints and chocolates can be taken out of their paper or cardboard boxes and spread out or heaped up in a basket. Place them in the living room, family room, or other area to which guests will retire after the meal. And few guests can resist a stack of homemade brownies nestled in a basket lined with waxed paper.

Besides food service, baskets are useful for other entertaining needs. When you are expecting visitors, stagger a few shallow baskets on the coffee table and stack photo albums featuring snapshots of your family on recent trips or ones taken of you and your guests enjoying a party or outing together. Be sure to include souvenirs that spark some of the best memories.

# eight sections, infinite uses

The sectioned basket is as versatile as its name implies. It serves up the crunchy crudités that accompany cocktails before dinner and is an efficient serving tray for a variety of pretzel rods, potato sticks, and cheese straws. When it's your week to host the bridge club, pour some chocolate-covered nuts and raisins in each section for a midgame treat.

This basket is indispensable for indoor housekeeping chores, and in the garage as well. To sort out your odds-and-ends drawer, try this quick organizer: Place a mason jar in each of the compartments, then fill the jars with whatever you find in the drawer—one with rubberbands; one with screws, tacks, and nails; another with twisty ties and chip clips.

## portable garden

As a centerpiece, each section can be occupied by a single vase or small bottle with one flower or a spray of flowers in it.

## happy birthday

Fill a basket with items that reflect the interests of the birthday's celebrant, whether the preferred hobby or sport is golfing or shopping, needlepointing or reading.

## cool tool caddy

Bring tools to the job—screwdrivers, folding tape measure, pliers, wire cutter, level—instead of bringing the job to the tools.

## car talk

There are few things that are more frustrating than being caught on the road with a problem in the car. Outfit a sectioned basket as an emergency kit with a fan belt, bottle of water, can of sand or cat litter (for being stuck in snow), and a can of compressed air that will fill your flat tire long enough to get to a garage.

## studio art

For the artist—whether working indoors or setting off for some open-air painting—the basket turns into a handy place to sort brushes, bottles of turpentine, charcoal, soft pencils, or oil paint.

## dressing table

Hand lotions, face creams, perfumes and eaux de cologne, manicure instruments, eye and lip pencils, and makeup brushes will all stand neatly inside the basket's compartments.

## show off

How better to show off your collection of vases, tumblers, antique bottles, or perfume atomizers?

## tea party

The eight-section basket is perfect for a child's tea-party set. Once the dishes have been washed and dried, they should be returned to their sections. Place the basket on an upper book-shelf where it will be safe and ready for the next tea party.

# two for the road

The market basket has a strong tradition in Europe. For generations, shoppers have carried their baskets each day to the market where they pick out what is freshest and—not incidentally—the best buy. Two different market baskets are popular in the United States: the bicycle basket and the backpack. One sunny day, put on your pack, and try shopping the European way.

Many of us are taking up cycling as a healthful activity, and a leisurely snack or drink halfway along the journey makes it all the more enjoyable. Bike baskets can carry enough gear for a few friends. And at the picnic they make the trip a snap. Traditional fare like crusty bread and rustic wine fit just as nicely as thermoses of steaming coffee and a box or two of biscotti.

# putting your best basket forward

Picnics are the great American pastime. The pleasures of bringing out favorite foods, enjoying the beach or a park, and relaxing in good weather are among life's greatest joys. The first step is finding a good hamper. Choose one carefully fitted with storage for just about anything you might need—corkscrew and bottle opener, salt and pepper shakers, glasses and cutlery, perhaps a telescope for some romantic late-night stargazing.

When preparing to head out for a picnic, most of us underestimate just how much we need to bring along, and before driving away we suddenly have accumulated a large variety of unwieldy odds and ends. We wind up with numerous grocery bags filled with bottles of sodas and water, grapes and other fragile fruits, an assortment of breads and cheeses, napkins and picnic blankets, cutting boards, maybe even a diary for an afternoon's musings. How much better to get organized with a basket designed for travel. The lid on this style of basket covers three-quarters of the interior, leaving the remaining compartment uncovered: the perfect place to stand a tall bottle of juice or crisp apple cider. All the necessities can be stowed within the hamper, so that only fresh food needs to be gathered at the last minute. Then, on a sunny weekend morning, let your sense of adventure guide you on a spontaneous trip to the park.

## car trip deluxe

If your family regularly takes long-distance trips to visit relatives and friends, the well-stocked picnic hamper can increase your travel pleasure immensely. Instead of relying on the typical fare of fast-food restaraunts, fill your hamper with the family's favorite lunch. Chances are you will probably save money, you'll all eat better, and you'll enjoy your trip that much more.

## dogs on the go

Planning a roadtrip or daytrip with man's best friend? A picnic basket is a tidy way to pack up all the necessities for your pet. A sleeping pad, frisbees, balls and other run-and-fetch toys, leashes and collars, bowls and dishes, fresh drinking water, and a stockpile of his or her favorite brand of bones and treats are travel essentials for the well-equipped canine.

# chapter three

# the organization specialists

EVEN THE MOST ORDERLY PEOPLE NEED BASKETS—FOR THEM, THE WHOLE WORLD

looks like something to organize. They constantly see new ways of arranging things more handily: grouping

them together, piling them up, stacking them on top of each other. They dream of containers for everything;

of matching like with like, size with size; of the right basket with the right purpose in the right space. For

those who are not inclined to be so neat, baskets have a way of organizing without being aggressive about it;

even the messiest child probably won't notice he's being corralled into order if he has baskets for all his

worldly possessions. Baskets somehow humanize the organizing process; they warm it up, make it friendly,

even make it likable. Substituting baskets for steel files, metal-edged footlockers, and cardboard boxes from

the supermarket is a smart and fun way to attain and enjoy the pleasures of an ordered life.

# home

## charms for modern living

Nothing contributes more to a look of chaos in the house than a jumble of sports equipment. When not in play, the skates that are part of a figure skater's elegance as he twirls on the ice or the swiftness of the hockey player as he speeds toward a goal are clumsy and space-consuming. So, too, the tennis racket that seemed as unsubstantial as a butterfly's wing as it was flashing above the court. In the typical home, the cry inevitably goes up at the start of a sports season—football, basketball, soccer, Saturday morning's softball or baseball game—"Where is my . . . ?" or "Who's seen my . . . ?" Then it's time for another archaeolog-ical dig through the unorganized storage closets or crowded trunks.

The solution to this perennial problem is a big sturdy basket like the kind that often holds a collection of toys. When it's time to set off for the snowy slopes, the frozen pond, the tennis court, or in-line skating path, baskets always answer the call for teamwork. Everyone knows exactly where to find what he or she needs.

As little children get bigger, there is a lot that baskets can teach them, in a very pleasant way, about order and taking care of their possessions. A medium-size basket becomes a good place to stow sneakers, rubber boots,

foul-weather hats, and a toy friend or two that likes nothing better than to go walking in the rain. A big basket turns into a portable library, ready for bedtime stories or teatime tales. Carry your children's book basket downstairs to the kitchen or family room so they can read while you work. A bit of space can usually be made at the table, too, for other necessities like magic markers and crayons, a thick pad of drawing paper, and a watercolor painting kit. Heap a big basket with board books and coloring books, and even a stuffed animal. Reading materials can be grabbed at the last minute, just before the school bus honks outside.

For older kids, baskets designated for higher-tech accessories such as video games, computer disks, and other components work like a charm. Choose baskets that can slide right onto a shelf.

# the personal touch

Big baskets set in or near the entrance of a house are handy for the daily flow of personal items in and out the door. A hallway or vestibule is a natural place for a utility basket large enough to store winter supplies of earmuffs, scarves, gloves, mittens, and hats. If space permits, a basket for each family member is an organizational luxury. One secret to the success of this type of entryway basket is regular tidying up: Keep gloves in pairs, fold scarves to prevent wrinkling, dry snowy caps before adding them to the basket. Also, on those days when the weather surprises you despite your careful research, same-size baskets at the doorway are handy as bins for ready-to-wear sweaters, windbreakers, and anoraks.

## for the bath

Individual baskets in the bathroom help keep towels and other bath linens organized. Be sure each family member and guest has a basket with his or her name on it. Or color-code the contents, one color per person.

## souvenirs

There are times in life when we want to remember every minute of a night at the theater, a trip to an exotic resort, or an extra-special weekend with a friend. Entrust a basket with your whole collection—matchbooks, playbills, local maps, as well as photographs of your happy time. It's even better than a scrapbook, because you can pick up and admire each item.

## sports practice

A basket with fruit juice or sports drink, a clean hand towel, a couple bandages, a few pieces of fruit, and an extra cap can make the difference between a good workout and a great one.

## beachcombers

If you love the beach, put seashells you find on your trips into baskets. You can set aside one for each of your favorite beaches, or divide the shells by type. Remember to include a separate basket for sea glass.

## mementos

Our children and grandchildren grow up before we know it. Collect items a child loves but outgrows, as well as the youngster's greeting cards and letters you've received, in a basket with a lid. Give the basket as a clever twenty-first birthday present or as a thoughtful wedding gift.

## hello again

Many of us are lucky enough to get repeat visits from relatives and friends. A separate basket for each visitor filled with hand-picked, personal items can be kept in the guest room closet and set out on the bedside table in anticipation of the visitor's arrival: what a personal welcome!

# toys, toys, and more toys

Thank goodness for baskets—they provide pretty, sturdy storage for a kid's toys, and they help children remember where to find and put back their precious belongings.

One mother told of her frustration at trying to organize her sons's room, until a light clicked on in her mind: baskets! She figured out how many she needed, then ordered twice that number. Once all of the baskets arrived, she and her boys had a lot of fun designing their room, and Mom reports that her sons since have been remarkable about keeping their toys and projects in order without her having to remind them.

Baskets can work as storage for a baby, a toddler, a preschooler, a seventh grader. Even teenagers can have baskets in their rooms without embarrassment, because there is no age factor associated with them. How many objects can we say that about?

Part of the fun kids have with baskets is personalizing them. Fine-quality baskets will hold up to roughhousing and hard play, not to mention being repeatedly stickered and painted and pasted up with photos of heartthrobs and sports heroes.

Baskets are ideal birthday and special-occasion gifts from one child to another. Once a basket is chosen, the child can go to a hobby or toy store and pick out small gifts for the lucky friend. Each gift can be wrapped individually and placed in the basket, which in turn can be tied with a bow and tagged with a handwritten card.

# six compartments, six ideas

A sectioned caddy basket—so good at bringing mustard, ketchup, salt, and pepper to the barbecue, or the honeys and jams to Sunday brunch—is remarkably adaptable to many organizational and toting tasks. It can compartmentalize everything needed to make baby's bath fun: powder, cotton swabs, shampoo, lotion, and a beloved toy standing ready in case of tears.

The sextuplet basket is also an ideal vehicle for the get-well gift. Look for the pampering extras that may do as much as medications to promote a speedy recovery: a sprightly pot of flowers, small linen towels, fine powders and lotions, perfume, and a slim volume of poetry.

## playtime pal

For the youngster who can't remain inactive long, the basket converts to a craft center with small-scale tools and materials for origami, wood carving, or cutting and pasting cardboard castles, cathedrals, or airplanes.

## setting the mood

The get-well basket for a child can be pretty and amusing. Tiny toys, such as miniature jigsaw puzzles and a chessboard, a windup toy, a bendable superhero figurine, or a snow dome paperweight might alternate with health-restoring packets of vitamin C, herbal tea, or lozenges.

## for the hostess

Today's hostess gift should say something about the giver as well as the recipient. One compartment might hold a glass jug of flowers; another a split of Champagne. Tuck some delicious chocolates into a third section, then add a board game, a pack of cards, and some photos of you and your hostess together at an earlier happy occasion.

## going away

If you have close neighbors or friends who are moving, say goodbye in a meaningful way with a caddy basket. In one section goes a compact disk you know they really like; in another, the local newspaper. If your favorite pastime together was croquet, include a hoop and a couple of brightly colored balls. Did you have a friendly rivalry about sports? Include two custom caps, one for each of your teams.

## crab feast

Have you ever been invited to a crab feast or another kind of food festival? How about a tailgate party before the game? Bring to the occasion a suitably equipped basket: plenty of newspapers, pliers, a hammer, and picks for the crab feast; glasses, straws, napkins, and placemats for the tailgate party.

## caddy shack

Think literal. If your buddy (or spouse) is a golf fanatic, stop at a pro-shop for balls, tees, gloves, a thermos for water, a towel for the golf bag, sunscreen, and a sun visor. Fore!

# gift wrapping station

Instead of jumbling all your gift wrappings in plastic bags in the linen closet or attic, create mobile gift wrapping stations with baskets. Wrapping gifts becomes a pleasant and organized endeavor when you sort and store materials by specific occasions on which you regularly give gifts—anniversaries, Father's Day, graduations, or Hannukah, for example. The baskets hold gift wrap and other necessities—scissors, tapes, spools of ribbon and twine, ornaments, gift tags. Another basket can store packing and shipping materials. When it's time to wrap, everything you need to make an eye-catching gift is at hand.

## baby gifts

Pretty paper decorated with sweet cherubs, pastel colored ribbons, extra tie-ons like baby rattles and gift tags the proud parents will want to save each go in their own section. You might want a bottle of ink and a calligrapher's pen to write your message of joy in a particularly beautiful script.

## for mother

How can we prepare an extra-special treat on Mother's Day? Use wrapping papers in their favorite colors, gather precious trinkets throughout the year, let them know you have really planned this present. Tie the box up with extravagant French wire ribbon. Best of all, mount a small photo of yourself as a child on the gift card, and inscribe a message of love and gratitude.

## office pals

Coworkers tend to form close bonds, and when one leaves, you can wrap a present that will long be remembered as the talk of the lunchroom or break room. Mimic ticker tape for ribbon, for example, and use ribbon to tie on an appropriate miniature charm such as a computer keyboard or cash register.

## birthdays

When the next birthday rolls around, coordinate the wrapping with the package inside. If you're giving a friend a luxurious aromatherapy candle, paste together magazine photographs of beautiful spa settings. Tie the package and secure the bow with a pretty box of matches and a stick of like-scented incense.

## weddings

Here's an event so romantic that you can't possibly go overboard. Choose a pale paper and several different kinds of ribbon. Prepare a gift tag with a poetic personal message that can go in the newlyweds' scrapbook, and add a nosegay of fresh stephanotis with a sheaf of wheat (a symbol of fertility) and a sprig of ivy (for the couple to plant in their garden).

## christmas

Several baskets may be required to hold all your holiday wrappings. Concentrate on paper and ribbons that complement each other. For final touches, have a good supply of pinecones, candy canes, Christmas ornaments, and a few sprigs of holly.

# hard at work at home

Baskets are so often used decoratively that it can be easy to forget that their primary jobs have been practical. Big, sturdy baskets have worked in textile mills to collect fabric scraps and to sort silk cocoons; in markets they have held vegetables, fruits, and even fish; and at the shoemaker's they receive shoes fresh from the cobbler's last.

In many cases, the jobs have changed, not the baskets. Today, laundry rarely flaps on clotheslines to dry in the sun. But the laundry basket is still around, carrying clothes to and from the washer and dryer. Since the openness of the basket's natural weave allows air to circulate, everything stays fresh, with no lingering moisture. The basket's naturally light weight makes toting the laundry less of a burden.

Definitely think of laundry baskets in multiples. Everyone should have at least one, plus a separate basket to keep dry cleaning sorted from laundry. Extra baskets work well for seasonal storage of curtains, towels, and bedding. Blankets can be put away for the summer (sprinkle cedar moth repellent between folds to keep those pesky insects away).

When it's not being pressed into service in the laundry room, the big basket is a great help when it's time for spring cleaning, clearing closets of outgrown clothes, single gloves, unwanted hats and caps, broken sports equipment, and discarded toys. A sidekick is good for storing the waxes, bleaches, cleaning products, and brushes often kept under the kitchen sink.

# workroom

## business and beyond

As offices and workplaces become more and more anonymous, employees put greater effort into making their niches their own. Personalizing space becomes a real necessity. Even in the most corporate environment, a simple wastepaper basket can also be a resting place for rolled-up blueprints, maps, promotional posters, drawings, or even a parking spot for your umbrella.

For a real office-warmer, take the drawers out of a metal filing cabinet and slide like-size rectangular baskets in to replace the drawers. Or if you don't have a filing cabinet, turn square baskets onto their sides and stack them vertically for open-front access to files, books, magazines, and other reference materials. A smaller basket stores and protects computer disks. Instead of plastic organizers in drawers that pull out from under the desktop, line up shallow baskets to hold extra desk keys, postage stamps, and letter openers. Split-ash baskets, with their unique beauty, go a long way to softening the often harsh look of the workplace, making the staff more comfortable and ultimately more productive.

At home, an office used by stay-at-home workers, weekend freelancers, and anyone managing the affairs of home and family might still fit the traditional definition. But increasingly, the home office just as often means a private place where we tend to our paperwork, menu planning, or hobbies. If you're not inclined to traditional filing systems, there are baskets that can help out—to hold cooking magazines and clipped recipes earmarked for a big holiday dinner; the rickrack, buttons, beads, and threads for your sewing project; or the very practical scissors, tapes, glue, and staple gun you need to implement a new decorating scheme. Perhaps one basket houses a bag or two of broken china and tiles for a future mosaic, or books with torn or missing pages and loose covers that are waiting to be mended and restored.

Home hobbyists approach their work quite intensely, taking great pains to keep equipment accessible and in good condition. Jewelry designers use many small baskets to hold different varieties of charms, pearls, wires, clasps, and chains with which to craft their goods. Baskets with handles are a natural for hobbyists, as they can be carried from one work site to another, and baskets with lids conceal unfinished projects at the end of the day.

Shallow baskets function well on worktops and desktops to organize and hold everything from the usual pencils, paper clips, rubber bands, and notepads to amenities such as candies or lollipops for visitors. And with plastic liners, baskets will shelter pots of golden crocuses, bundles of fragrant honeysuckle, or small branches of winterberry or palm fronds.

# baskets help you

Create a basket plan that's tailored to your entire family's needs. If your child is a gymnast, devote a basket to the training equipment and clothing the sport requires. Or use baskets to organize all those notes, lists, and plans for the annual church bake sale that you've volunteered to run. Labels help keep the baskets neat and orderly.

## reminders

Place your important notes in a to-do basket for easy reference and accessibility: telephone message pads for recording the numbers of people who have called, e-mails that require follow-up responses, and the all-important daily planner.

## home records

Here's a way to keep track of household utility bills so they can be located promptly. Stay on top of the telephone company, gas and electric utility, and cable service each month.

## business cards

Choose a small basket to store those stacks of business cards you're handed each week from colleagues, suppliers, and service people.

## stationery

Personal and business stationery may include letterheads, envelopes, business cards, perhaps invoices, and various forms. Keep your social life and business activities separate, with baskets devoted to each.

## school stuff

Report cards, health forms, weekly menus, notices about field trips—school communications seem never ending. Toss it all in a basket for each of your kids, then sort out the keepers from the disposable notes once every month.

## medical records

Mailboxes today are bursting with notices from insurance companies, HMO's, test laboratories, and doctors' offices. Put all health-care paperwork into a basket to keep it at hand and under control until you have time to review it. Don't forget to keep a separate basket for your pet's records!

## auto basket

Your car needs tires rotated, oil changed, a new headlight bulb. Keep track of auto expenses and services with a basket for all those receipts and warranties.

## appliances

Keep warranties and registration cards for all your purchases, from the answering machine to the refrigerator, in a single basket. It's also a good place to keep instruction manuals for new appliances and electronics.

Every home needs a correspondence basket. Even in this age of computers and e-mail, we still have the occassional old-fashioned letter to write, whether it's a note to the editor of the local newspaper or simply a postcard to an old friend. Immediately putting each piece of paper in a designated basket as soon as it comes in guarantees that it won't go astray. Another, larger basket can accommodate the catalogs with which we're all inundated these days. A third basket can hold greeting cards and invitations.

Those of us who are lucky enough to have a sheltered front porch can mount a flat-back basket on the front door for mail and messages. If you're going out to an appointment, simply clothespin a note penned to the letter carrier, delivery person, or family member stating when you'll be back.

# chapter four

# special

# occasions

EVERY YEAR CAN BE ENRICHED WITH OCCASIONS MADE MORE MEMORABLE STILL by baskets: baskets of gifts, baskets for the glamorous picnic, baskets for the beautiful wedding, beribboned baskets for holding souvenir slices of wedding cake to take home. There can be baskets to surprise and please the children, baskets to hide away the presents, baskets to present the presents, baskets to give and get back again. The occasions seem almost limitless: A New Year's Eve basket by the door offers party hats and noise-makers to guests. The birthday basket overflows with an assortment of the birthday person's favorite things, from miniature boxes of chocolates and packets of exotic coffees to jams and jellies with matching spoons. An anniversary basket, with a dear note attached, conceals a bottle of Champagne and two glasses. If there isn't an occasion marked on the calendar, simply create your own.

# easter

## symbols of spring

One of the nicest aspects of Easter is its arrival in early spring, when the cold winds of winter, the sudden snowstorms, and the ice are past. Armed with a basket, home gardeners inspect the yard, clearing away leaves that have blanketed the plants, giving the green tips of bulbs their chance. Indoors, baskets of bright and fragrant flowers—hyacinths, daffodils, lilies—dominate the house. The dining room table, the sideboard, the hall—each holds its own little bouquet. The kitchen windowsill is lined with baskets of pansies. Single baskets of tulips and muscari climb the stairs. A basket of spring blossoms or bulbs sits on every

bedside table while crocuses stand by every bathroom sink. Even the nursery has little baskets of forget-me-nots or violets atop the dresser, all leading up to the celebration of Easter.

Before the holiday, the kitchen transforms itself into a magical work-place, sharp with the aroma of vinegar. Adults and children gather to dye and decorate hard-cooked or hollowed eggs. A big basket offers the eggs; smaller ones hold dyes, cartoonlike transfers, wax pencils, bits of gold paper, pretty lace, or ribbon to paste on the eggs, cardboard collars for them to sit in. Another basket presents refreshments for the workers: sugar cookies or fresh

strawberries. Once the eggs have been elegantly transformed, they are whisked away in baskets to be hidden in closets, the garden, or cupboards, awaiting discovery on Easter morning.

The celebration spreads beyond the house—in the trees hung with pastel eggs, all over the lawn, perhaps even in the sky, if the sun is shining and a stream of bubbles blown by a child floats in a leisurely fashion overhead. A basket of flowers—lilies-of-the-valley and pussy willow, or an extravagantly blooming azalea—may stand in welcome on the porch or by the door.

In the hall, dressed-up baskets of gifts are viewed with excited speculation by the children as they come downstairs. Inside, eggs, bunnies, yellow chicks, and small presents vie for attention with rabbit-shaped cookies prettily iced and inscribed with each child's name.

For the best treat of all, colored eggs, chocolate eggs and rabbits, jelly beans, and marshmallow chicks nestle in green cellophane grass, comprising the traditional Easter basket.

A centerpiece of holiday flowers, whether daffodils, primroses, or parrot tulips, underscores the joy of the day. The basket motif can be continued by serving side dishes in casseroles tucked into baskets. A tiny basket with a handwritten tag should mark each place setting; inside, it might contain a cross and a chocolate lamb to symbolize the Easter resurrection.

Later, the whole family, including young boys in new suits and little girls in their pretty coats and hats—may take baskets of flowers, cookies, and colored eggs to friends. Truly, the basket epitomizes the spirit of the holiday: a container of hope, health, and renewal.

# summer days of bounty & ease

Summertime—and the living is easy. These are the days when the question of the moment is shall we eat in the dining room, on the porch, or in the garden? Or should we just go on a picnic? We crave food that's light, quick to prepare, and easy to serve. By turning to your pantry of baskets, you can accommodate your family's last-minute dinner plans in seconds.

For outdoor activities and entertaining, keep baskets of various sizes on hand—a tall crowd-pleasing cooler for cold drinks to hand out at the softball game or a small basket for snacks on the patio. For picnics, look for hampers with generous and well-planned compartments so food and drinks will remain standing safely upright.

# giving and receiving

A thoughtful gesture is always appreciated. Good friends often trade favors, favorite items, little gifts throughout the year. How much more fun to exchange these gifts, talents, and bounty in a "sharing basket." If you are an irrepressible baker, send gifts from your oven to your best friend in a basket with a lid. In return, she may send back the basket to you with new recipes or vintage kitchen utensils and dish towels. If one of you is an avid gardener, fill the basket with flowering bulbs or seedlings. Over the years, the basket will come to represent the affection and generosity both of you share.

## a stitch in time

For the seamstress or quilter, fill a lidded basket with a pretty assortment of fabrics, pins, scissors, and thimbles. Even unwieldy items such as pin cushions, large spools of thread, and jumbo balls of colored yarn fit neatly inside.

## for book lovers

Do you and your friend adore mysteries? Romances? Biographies? Whatever your favorite books, pass them between you in a basket that can be refilled with new ones every week or so. Include book reviews and articles from the newspaper or weekly magazines.

## video carrier

Home videos are made to be watched over and over: the wedding, baby's first steps, a birthday dinner. Even videos of favorite movies can be traded back and forth in a good basket.

## hand-me-downs

If your children are close in age, exchange outgrown or too-big clothes, sneakers, and sports gear. You and your friend will save hours of shopping for seasonal items like baseball batting gloves, hockey skates, ski pants, and swimsuits.

## coupon clippers

Diligent coupon clippers know that they can substantially reduce their food expenses each week with the right coupons. Clip coupons for products that aren't on your shopping list but that your friend would like to have. And if there's only one coupon allowed per family, pass along the extra one for her.

## forget-me-nots

We visit a friend and don't remember to take home the magazine article, vacation photos, the new nail polish we brought to share. Luckily, it works both ways: You can return your friend's forgotten keys, cellular phone, or notebook in a round-trip basket.

# halloween

## trick-or-treat stash

Little Red Riding Hood had one. So did Dorothy in *The Wizard of Oz*. Many of our favorite characters have baskets as part of their ensembles. On Halloween, the effect of a hilarious or beautiful costume can be diminished when the trick-or-treater presents a plastic bag or pillowcase for the treat.

What's the solution for a well-dressed reveler? An easy-to-carry basket with a handle is a charming accessory for any goblin or ghoul. The basket's solid sides and bottom protect the sugary goodies within. When the All-Hallow's-Eve round of the neighborhood is over and it's time to empty the basket onto the table and count out the treats that have been collected, none of them will be crushed, bruised, or otherwise damaged.

For a truly spooky effect, line your darkened sidewalk, porch, or driveway with baskets and stand a lighted candle in a clear-glass holder in each one. Always put safety first by carefully choosing candle sizes that are well-suited to your baskets to avoid the threat of damaging them. Or if you're not planning on being at home while the children make their way from door to door, leave a basket filled with a multitude of bite-size candy bars, chewing gum, and lollipops on the front steps or just outside the door.

Many communities are replacing traditional door-to-door trick-or-treating with Halloween parties for the whole neighborhood. Everyone is invited, whether they have children or not, and everyone, including Mom and Dad and even some of the best-behaved pets, wears a costume. Prizes are awarded for the most authentic, most imaginative, and funniest get-ups. Guests pitch in by bringing pot-luck treats for the gang—luscious cupcakes, caramel popcorn balls, and taffy apples. Transport them intact in a basket with a lid, and tuck in tiny packets of candy corn to be taken home by each youngster after the big party.

# thanksgiving

## horns of plenty

Thanksgiving is the holiday we most associate with food, home, and hearth. For many Americans, this is a favorite holiday, perhaps because it seems free from commercialism, a pure celebration that takes note of our daily bounty. America has always been blessed with an abundance of natural riches and new opportunities, and it seems only fitting that such wealth be noted and appreciated each year.

The Puritans who participated in the first Thanksgiving brought offerings in baskets; that tradition can be carried on today. Gourds fresh from the garden or ears of Indian corn, with their jewel-like colors, make stunning displays. Newly popular miniature pumpkins are charming piled into a basket. Tiny baskets filled with fresh cranberries can be part of each place setting. Or use acorns instead of cranberries and line them up along the windowsills. A mantel basket holds an extravagant display of autumn leaves, bittersweet, curly willow, and bramble. Centerpiece baskets of sheafs of wheat and stems of sumac are at home on side tables and coffee tables around the house. From the diminutive to the grand, baskets still play a part in this well-loved celebration.

# christmas

## good cheer and goodwill to all

Christmas always means baskets full of lush seasonal greens and pinecones, tall pillar candles, and holiday ornaments. A single-handled basket brimming with a collection of antique Santas enchants family and guests alike. A nativity scene might be arranged in a flat flower-gathering basket and placed on a table or under the tree. A mail basket on the hallway wall holds the wealth of Christmas cards you've received.

Christmas baskets offer endless opportunities for hospitality: flowering bulbs in each bedroom and bathroom; poinsettias in the entry, on the piano, and on the kitchen counter. A pyramid of oranges studded with whole cloves in decorative patterns makes a holiday basket that smells as good as it looks. If your family likes Christmas crackers—the kind you pull apart to find the surprise inside—pile dozens of them into a long basket. Choose a caddy basket to hold bottles containing different kinds of evergreen branches.

For entertaining drop-in guests, improvise a bar in a sectioned basket, with different kinds of liquors and mixers in each compartment. Offer guests refreshments in a punch bowl basket and pass around baskets of nuts, candies, and spicy gingerbread.

# a year of baskets

BASKETS HAVE BECOME SO MUCH A PART OF OUR DAILY LIFE THAT WE NOTICE if they aren't there. When you're visiting a home for the first time, have you ever had the feeling that something was missing, that something was just slightly off? You were probably in a room lacking a plant, books, or a basket of any kind. There is no single style of interior design that cannot be complemented or warmed up with baskets. And baskets have the versatility to play many roles throughout the year.

Invent new uses for baskets, trying the most unusual, the most practical, and the most outrageous displays you can conjure. One tradition is to create a special basket for each month of the year. Fresh fruits, flowering plants, tree branches, and all kinds of natural elements are the first step in designing seasonal baskets. But beyond Nature's bounty, there is a world of interesting choices: firewood for January chills; popcorn for watching the Academy Awards in March; knitted wool gloves and scarves in November; cut-out hearts for Valentine's Day; and, of course, baskets, baskets, and even more baskets of presents in December.

january  february

march  april

may

june

july

august

september october

november december

# baskets
# page by page

# care & cleaning

THE BEST CARE YOU CAN GIVE TO A BASKET IS TO LET IT REMAIN IN AS NATURAL A state as possible. Enjoy it every day, and it will remain flawless if you keep it away from the drying heat of oven, stove, radiator, or sun. A basket cannot tolerate extreme conditions: heat, cold, wet, dry. However, if you keep it in an area where it has constant exposure to gentle humidity, the quality of the basket will be maintained over the years. A well-ventilated (not damp) bathroom with a tub or shower, for instance, is a good place to store a basket. Or if you have a porch or gazebo, set your basket outside under the shelter during a warm summer shower; the basket will actually drink up its share of the moisture from the stormy air.

Though the dyes and stains on Peterboro baskets are always food-compatible, it's just as well to avoid putting food directly in a basket without a clean napkin or plastic cloth around it. Carefully tack the fabric in as a permanent lining with a needle and thread if a cleaner look is more your style.

All Peterboro baskets are guaranteed for life but may need some occasional TLC. If a spill or other accident does occur and you feel the basket must be cleaned, do not immerse it in water. Instead, begin by preparing a solution of warm water and a mild liquid cleaner, such as Murphy Oil Soap. Dip a soft, clean cloth—an eyeglass cleaning cloth is ideal because of its smooth, nonabrasive texture—into the solution. Wring the cloth gently to remove the excess water—the cloth should be damp, not dripping. Gently rub the cloth over the weave of the basket. Thoroughly clean the inside as well as the exterior. Then dry the basket with another soft cloth that is clean and absorbent, and allow it to air dry fully before reusing or storing it. If you need it to dry quickly, you may blow your basket dry using a hairdryer on a no-heat setting or a cool oscillating fan. If the problem is a simple accumulation of dust, you can clean the basket with the same soft cloth, skipping the soap, water, and drying rubdown.

To order Peterboro Baskets
call 1-800-345-1515 or visit www.qvc.com